STOIC SPIRITUAL EXERCISES
Elen Buzaré

In this short essay, Elen Buzaré examines ancient sources for clues to how Stoics of the Roman era used psychological techniques for turning doctrine into practical daily living, securing for themselves lives that flourished, free from troubles, enjoying an unshakeable peace of mind.

With the help of this short guide, modern readers can similarly train themselves to live as Stoics, making progress towards the same 'good flow of life' and serenity, and develop a mindfulness that is immune to all harm, joyous in response to all that fate might bring.

Especially suited to those who have already introduced themselves to the basics of Stoic doctrine, this little book will serve as inspiration and guide for anyone wanting to advance further on the Stoic way.

Elen Buzaré has devoted herself to deepening her understanding of Stoic philosophy from the age of 20. She now works for an insurance broking company in Lyon, France.

STOIC
SPIRITUAL EXERCISES

Elen Buzaré

LULU

Stoic Spiritual Exercises

First published 2011
by Lulu
www.lulu.com

© 2011 Elen Buzaré

Typeset in Minion Pro 12/17 pt

All rights reserved. No part of this book may be reprinted or reproduced or utilised in any form or by any electronic, mechanical, or other means, now known or hereafter invented, including photocopying and recording, or in any information storage or retrieval system, without permission in writing from the publisher.

ISBN 978–1–4466–0811–1 (hardback)
ISBN 978–1–4466–0813–5 (paperback)

In memory of Pierre Hadot
(1922–2010)

Do not stop sculpting your own statue.
—*Plotinus*

Contents

I   The different ways of meditating

   A The memorisation exercise (*mnêmê*)   19
      1 The writing meditation (*hypomnêmata*) 23
         – getting started   24
      2 Self-examination exercise   25
         – deepening your understanding   27
   B *Prosochê* or the art of attention   27

II   The Exercises as continual applications of Logic, Physics and Ethics

   A Practical logic
      1 The discipline of judgement   32
      2 The *aproptôsia* or *epochê* exercise   37
   B Practical Physics
      1 The discipline of desire (and aversion)   39
      2 Examples of *epilegein* in desire
         a *Praemeditation malorum*   41
           – deepening your understanding   44
         b Physical definition   46
         c Restitution   49
         d Impermanence or universal metamorphosis   50

		e	Wand of Hermes	52
		f	Self-expansion into the world	54
		g	View from above	57
	C	Practical Ethics		
		1	The discipline of impulse	59
		2	Examples of *epilegein* in impulse	
			a Defining the planned action	63
			b Acting 'with reservation'	66
			c Acting for the good of the community	69
			d Acting according to value (*kat' axian*)	72

III Attempt to reconstruct a Stoic meditation

A	The help of Buddhist Samatha-Vipassyana therapy		77
B	The help of the Hesychastic Prayer tradition		80
	1	To meditate like a mountain (*hexis*)	82
	2	To meditate like a poppy (*phusis*)	83
	3	To mediate like an ocean (*psuchê*)	84
	4	To meditate like a Sage (*nous*)	85

IV Concluding thoughts 89

P HILOSOPHERS OF THE HELLENISTIC period see philosophy as having the practical purpose of guiding people towards leading better lives. The aim was to secure for oneself *eudaimonia*, and the different schools and philosophers of the period offered differing solutions as to how the *eudaimôn* life was to be won.

The meaning of *eudaimonia* is not that well conveyed by the English term 'happiness', which is commonly the term used in contemporary translations. In fact, as Keith Seddon succinctly puts it:

> *Eudaimonia* means 'supremely blessed', and conveys the notion of someone who is flourishing fully, someone who is happy not just in the sense that they are having a good time, or enjoying some temporary

pleasure, but whose happiness is of a special kind: it is stable and enduring, it is a persistence of flourishing that pervades their whole life. Zeno defines it as a 'good flow of life' (*euroia biou*).[1]

It is readily evident that, alas, few people are content with their lives, certainly not in any sustained or permanent fashion. In the language of the ancient philosophers, we can make the bold (but nevertheless honest) claim that if anyone ever does enjoy *endaimonia*, that will be the rarest of phemonena.

In the course of daily life, we are beset by frustrations and setbacks of every conceivable type. Our cherished enterprises are hindered and thwarted, we have to deal with hostile and offensive people, and we have to cope with the difficulties and anxieties occasioned by the setbacks and illnesses visited upon our friends and relations. Sometimes, we are ill ourselves, and even those who have the good fortune to enjoy sound health have to face the fact of their own mortality. In the midst of all this, only the rare few are blessed with lasting and rewarding relationships, and even these

---

[1] Keith Seddon, *Epictetus' Handbook and the Tablet of Cebes* (London: Routledge, 2005), 33.

relationships, along with everything that constitutes human life, are wholly transient.²

There is a good reason for this state of affairs. According to Epictetus, this situation results from mistaken beliefs about what is truly good. We have invested our hope in the wrong things, or at least invested it in the wrong way.

We can remedy this by understanding that our capacity to flourish and be happy is entirely dependent upon how we dispose ourselves to ourselves, to others, and to events generally. Therefore, our capacity to be *eudaimôn* is entirely up to us.

Keith Seddon continues:

> The central claim of Stoic ethics is that only the virtues and virtuous activities are good, and that the only evil is vice and actions motivated by vice. When someone pursues pleasure or wealth, say, believing these things to be good, the Stoics hold that this person has made a mistake with respect to the nature of the thing pursued and the nature of their own being, for the Stoics deny that advantages such as pleasure and health (wealth and status, and so forth) are *good*, because they do not benefit those who possess them

---

² Seddon, *Epictetus' Handbook*, 9.

in all circumstances. Virtue, on the other hand, conceived as the capacity to use such advantages wisely, being the only candidate for that which is always beneficial, is held to be the only good thing. Thus the Stoics identify the *eudaimôn* ('happy') life as one that is motivated by virtue.[3]

If, as explained above, the goal of philosophy is to guide people towards leading better lives, there should be a link between philosophy and virtue.

Indeed, Stoic definitions of philosophy may appear dissimilar at first view, but they are in reality very close to each other. According to Seneca,[4] 'some said that it consisted in exercising oneself to virtue (*studium virtutis*), others that it was to exercise oneself to correct our mind (*studium corrigendae mentis*) and consequently, some inferred that it was the search for correct reasoning (*adpetitio rectae rationis*).'

In concrete terms, philosophy consists in exercising virtue. Virtue, which constitutes the excellence or nobility (*aretê*) of a human life, is also the *psyche's health*. Zeno chose to say that virtue consists in 'living in accordance' (*to homologoumenôs*

---

[3] Seddon, *Epictetus' Handbook*, 10.
[4] *Moral Epistle* 89.

zên) where the Greek can be understood as both the accordance of each of us with the *logos* and the accordance of reason with itself, that is free of passions.

Virtue is also generally considered as being a science (*epistêmê*), which means full comprehension of a certain number of notions, which forms a coherent and true system. What ancient Stoics tried to explain by using the term *full comprehension* was that a virtue should not be grasped only through mere intellectual investigation but also through *incorporation of the experience*.

According to Stoicism, each of us is our own therapist. For the ancients the term *therapeutès* had two meanings. It can be translated as either 'to serve, to take care, to worship' or 'to cure'. Indeed, Marcus Aurelius[5] says that a man should not fail 'to hold fast to the guardian spirit within him and serve it single-mindedly' (*pros nomô tô endon eauton daimoni einai kai touton gnêsiôs therapeuein*). So ancient Stoics also practised medicine (*iatrikê*) but their profession was superior to the one usually practised in cities, which only cures bodies, for they also aimed at curing the psyche when the latter was prey to harsh illnesses called passions.

---

[5] *Meditations* 2.13.

All of this is very interesting, but it does not explain how we should proceed to be virtuous, to develop a healthy mind and behaviour.

Every Hellenistic school of philosophy, including the Stoics, had their own spiritual exercises (*askêsis, meletê*), that is, personal and voluntary practices designed to bring about an inner transformation. Despite the fact that many texts refer to these exercises, no systematic treatise exhaustively codifies a theory of *askêsis* and practice, for this teaching was probably transmitted orally. However, Pierre Hadot maintains that some treatises on such exercises existed which are now lost.[6]

We know little about ancient Stoic practices: In fact, only a helpful little treatise written by Musonius Rufus[7] has survived in which he distinguishes two main categories of exercise.

First, exercises peculiar to the soul. This first category is itself divided into two subsections:

(1) Those exercises consisting in always keeping in mind (or meditating upon) the school's fundamental teachings which aim at developing a different outlook upon things. Here, the ancient Stoics re-

---

[6] Pierre Hadot, *What is Ancient Philosophy?* (Cambridge, MA: Belknap Press of Harvard University Press, 2002), 135.

[7] In A-J Festugière, *Deux prédicateurs de l'Antiquité : Télès et Musonius* (Paris: Vrin, 1978), 69–71.

quired their students to learn by rote a summary of their doctrines in the form of short sentences logically and harmoniously linked together. Among the other schools of philosophy, Stoics were famed for their rigor in this.

(2) Those exercises consisting in examining the purity of intention. What I call the *'aproptôsia'* exercises are a good example of this (see page 37, below).

Secondly, exercises peculiar to both the soul and the body. The goal of this second category of exercise is to get used to cold, heat, hunger, frugal food, an uncomfortable bed, and so forth. In doing so, the student's body becomes insensitive to pain, and consequently the soul itself is fortified and becomes courageous, disciplined and ready for action.

Hadot stresses the idea that these thoughts from Musonius are precious because they show that the notion of philosophical exercises has its roots in the ideal of athleticism and in the habitual practice of physical training typical of the gymnasia:

> Just as the athlete gave new strength and form to his body by means of repeated bodily exercises, so the philosopher developed his strength of soul by means of philosophical exercises, and transforms himself. ...

Exercises of body and soul thus combined to shape the true person: free, strong, and independent.[8]

This essay will focus on the first category of exercise, that is, those peculiar to the soul.

However, I do not underestimate the value of the second category of exercise, for it is obviously difficult to resist different kinds of desires if, for instance, one never leaves the security of a cosy house or has always been accustomed to expensive food, or the luxury of beautiful and warm clothes. Stoic tradition has always strongly promoted living simply (with respect to food, shelter, clothes, and so forth) in order that we should remain free from accumulation of power, knowledge and possessions that may entice us away from Nature.

There may be real value in practising such exercises today. I would nevertheless urge modern Stoics to seek advice from their physician before undertaking exercises along these lines, because there are potential dangers in engaging in demanding training to which one is not accustomed.

However, I think that a good beginning would be to regularly practise some form of physical exercise, along with a healthy diet. I personally chose to

---

[8] Hadot, *What is Ancient Philosophy?* 189.

practise the Original Pilates Method, for it is both a meditation and a way of strengthening the body.

Whatever may be your choice, you should never forget that being a *therapeutês* implies that you have to *take care of yourself* and not to harm your body through unwise training that would bring you nothing.

This essay will, first, describe the different ways of meditation within the Stoic tradition. Secondly, it will develop Pierre Hadot's theory that Stoic exercises are in fact the constant application of Logic, Physics and Ethics, before finally trying an attempt to reconstruct a form of Stoic meditation.

I The different ways of meditating

Pierre Hadot[9] has made an approximate reconstruction of the way Stoic philosophers used to meditate. Such a reconstruction is difficult, although not impossible, because of the lack of sources. Nevertheless, he has been able to distinguish, as far as Stoics are concerned, the writing meditation (*hypomnêmata*) from the self-attention or mindfulness exercise (*prosochê*).

A The memorisation exercise (*mnêmê*)

Stoics have always drawn to their students' attention the necessity to keep 'right at hand' (*procheiron*) their fundamental teachings.

The goal is to get accustomed to the rules of life (*kanôn*) by applying them to everyday circumstances, in a very similar way to that in which one

---

[9] Pierre Hadot, *Qu'est ce que la philosophie antique?* (folio essais, Gallimard, 1995). This book has been translated into English under the title *Philosophy as a Way of Life*.

assimilates a rule of grammar by applying it to particular cases.

However, the issue here is not to acquire a theoretical knowledge. As John Sellars eloquently puts it:

> To become a student of philosophy in antiquity did not mean merely to learn a series of complex arguments or engage in intellectual debate. Rather, it involved engaging in a process of transforming one's character (*êthos*) and soul (*psuchê*), a transformation that would itself transform one's way of life (*bios*).[10]

The aim, then, is to formulate to oneself a rule of life in the most dynamic and concrete way, to put 'before ones eyes' the circumstances one is experiencing in the light of this rule.

Students of Stoicism were provided with such 'right at hand' maxims, very much like formulas or persuasive argumentations (*epilogismoi*), such as the *tetrapharmakos*, or fourfold remedy (adopted by Epicurus and his followers):

---

[10] John Sellars, *The Art of Living: The Stoics on the Nature and Function of Philosophy* (Bristol: Bristol Classical Press, 2nd edition, 2009), 23.

(1) *Gods are not to be feared;* (2) *death is not to be dreaded;* (3) *what is good is easy to acquire;* (4) *what is bad is easy to bear.*[11]

Arrian's *Handbook* of Epictetus, or *Encheiridion*, is another good example of a set of easy-to-learn short formulas, but many other persuasive arguments may be rediscovered through a careful reading of Marcus Aurelius' *Meditations* (*ta eis heauton*) such as this one:

The soul of man does violence to itself above all when it becomes, so far as it can, an abscess and a sort of morbid outgrowth on the universe. For to set your mind against anything that comes to pass is to set yourself apart from nature, which embraces as part of itself the nature of all individual things.

Again, it does violence to itself

(1) when it turns away from any other person, or

(2) moves against him with the intention of causing him harm, as it is the case with those who lose their temper; and

(3) thirdly, when it is overcome by pleasure or pain; and

---

[11] Philodemus in Herculaneum Papyrus 1005, col 5, 9–14.

(4) fourthly, when it dissimulates, and says or does something under false pretences; and

(5) fifthly, when failing to direct any act or impulse of its own towards a definite mark, it embarks on anything whatever in an aimless and ill-considered manner, although even the least of its actions should be performed in reference to an end; and the end for rational creatures is this, to conform to the reason and law of the most venerable of cities and constitutions.[12]

This exercise of memorising short maxims requires constant input: that is, it requires the understanding of the theoretical basis which justifies any specific rule of life. It is therefore very important not to discard the intellectual study of Stoic theory through the reading of philosophical texts, whether these are books written by contemporary scholars, or texts written by ancient or modern Stoics themselves. The ancients had also developed a classification of exercises corresponding to the study of philosophical discourses (*logos*): reading, audition (*akroasis*), research (*zêtêsis*), deep examination (*skepsis*).

---

[12] *Meditations* 2 16 (trans. Hard, typographically modified).

I shall detail below two examples of how maxims or short formulas may be used: the writing meditation and the self-examination.

1   THE WRITING MEDITATION (OR *HYPOMNÊMATA*)

Pierre Hadot[13] has shown that the writing meditation was a spiritual exercise in itself, especially for the Stoics of the imperial era.

As I explained above, ancient Stoics advised their students, day and night, to recall to mind their doctrines with the help of summaries composed as memorable maxims. Students were probably asked to write their own journal, using the given summaries as models and starting points.

Marcus Aurelius' *Meditations* should be understood in this way. In his work, the Emperor formulates for himself the dogmas of Stoicism. However, it is not enough merely to re-read his words. On the contrary, the important thing is to continuously reformulate the doctrines and the sentences which invite action of a particular character. What is really

---

[13] Pierre Hadot, *Exercices spirituels et philosophie antique* (Paris: Etudes augustiniennes, 1987).

important is the art of writing, understood in this context as the art of speaking to oneself.

The writing meditation is not a summary like a mathematical formula that one should re-read and apply mechanically whenever one so pleases. Its aim is not to solve abstract and theoretical questions, but to put oneself in such a situation that one feels obliged to live as a Stoic. This is why Marcus Aurelius so many times appears to repeat the same thing in various ways in his *Meditations*, as you have probably noticed.

This form of exercise is typically Stoic, and its use extended through the centuries. In his Exercises (or *Askêmata*), Anthony Ashley Cooper, Third Earl of Shaftesbury, a modern Stoic living into the eighteenth century, still respects this tradition.

Getting started: write down your own *hypomnêmata*

- Please take a good translation of Marcus Aurelius' *Meditations* and try to isolate the fundamental points hidden behind Marcus' literary style in the following chapters: 2.1, 2.6, 4.3, 4.26, 7.22, 8.21, 11.18, 12.7, 12.8 and 12.26

- Learn by rote these fundamental points in the form of laconic *aide mémoire*

- Take a sheet of paper, or a notebook, then write down these fundamental points at any convenient moment, embroidering them with your own style. You can choose either to reconstruct the whole argument, or focus on a specific point

2 SELF-EXAMINATION EXERCISE

Self-examination is a key feature in the Stoic programme of self-development. Seneca writes:

> [One's mind] should be summoned each day to give account of itself. Sextius used to do this. At the day's end, when he had retired for the night, he would interrogate his mind: 'What ailment of yours have you cured today? What failing have you resisted? Where can you show improvement? ... Could anything be finer than this habit of sifting through the whole day? Think of the sleep that follows the self-examination! How calm, deep, and unimpeded it must be, when the mind has been praised or admonished and—its

own sentinel and censor—has taken stock secretly of its own habits.[14]

Epictetus also refers to this exercise, quoting one of Pythagoras' golden verse in his *Discourse* 3.10.3:

> Do not let sleep fall upon your soft eyes
> Before you have gone over each act of your day
>   three times:
> Where have I failed? What have I done? What duty
>   have I omitted?
> Begin here, and continue the examination. After
>   this
> Find fault with what was badly done, and rejoice in
>   what was good.[15]

This is a good exercise to do just before going to bed. Buddhists, who practise a similar exercise, tend to think that it contributes to sleeping well.

If you feel disappointed by your lack of progress dealing with other people, suffering a loss or facing setbacks and suchlike, try to think of what Seneca or

---

[14] Seneca, *On Anger* 3.36 1–3, trans. John M. Cooper and J. F. Procopé, *Seneca: Moral and Political Essays* (Cambridge: Cambridge University Press, 1995), 110.
[15] trans. Pierre Hadot, *What is Ancient Philosophy?* (Harvard: Harvard University Press, 2004), 199–200.

Epictetus or Marcus Aurelius would have done, or what indeed they would have said to you.

As much as you must be honest with yourself about your faults, you must also not forget to acknowledge your achievements.

📖 Deepening your understanding

- This practice of 'self-examination' goes with another one. Every morning, remind yourself of your determination to apply Stoic principles throughout the coming day. Rejoice in still being alive — you could, after all, have died during the night — and be happy to be granted a new day in which to become a better Stoic

B *Prosochê* or the art of attention

Prosochê is the exercise of self-attention or mindfulness. It is a form of mental development by which we progressively learn to be attentive to every single action, thought or sensation we may have or feel at the very time they appear.

Of course, developing this ability requires some

training using appropriate techniques. Indeed, whether you are walking, sitting down, standing up, crouching, sleeping, eating, drinking, and so on, you should be fully conscious of what you are doing. This means that you should live in your present action. This does not mean that you should forget about the past and the future. On the contrary, you have to think about other times, but in relation to the present, and your present action, and when it is necessary to do so.

This idea is well rendered by one of the Stoic conceptions of the present, in which the present is defined in relation to the person's consciousness which perceives it and the degree of attention applied to it. From this point of view, the present has a certain duration, a certain 'density' which may be more or less large (*kata platos*).

Prosoché does not mean that you should actually think: 'I am doing this' or 'I am doing that.' The danger in thinking 'I am doing this' arises when you become conscious of yourself and, consequently, you do not live in the action but in the idea of 'I am.'

The same attention should be applied to every feeling or sensation you may have. In fact you should be able to observe yourself as a scientist would.

It is strange to note that a person who gets angry

usually does not realise that she is angry. As soon as someone makes her realise her emotion, she becomes quieter and often somewhat uneasy. Attention to thoughts and sensations is, I think, the most difficult to practise.

The ancients generally defined the psyche in terms of activity, as 'that which moves itself'. Hence, the *hêgemonikon*—sometimes called *nous* or *daimon* by ancient Stoics, as Pierre Hadot demonstrated—gives rise to good or bad thoughts and emotions in response to various kinds of impressions. These may be qualified as 'movements of the soul'.

With reference to the uneducated person, the *hêgemonikon* can be qualified as being *aeikinetos kai polukinetos*, which means 'always and extremely agitated'. Thus, the uneducated person is not likely to control the multiple passions that may arise if she is not able to pacify her *psuchê*.

As Epictetus explained:

> The soul is like a vessel filled with water; and impressions are like a ray of light that falls upon the water. If the water is disturbed, the ray will seem to be disturbed likewise, though in reality it is not. Whenever, therefore, a man is seized with vertigo, it is not the arts and virtues that are confounded, but the spirit in

which they exist; and, if this comes to rest, so will they likewise.[16]

Developing attention, which cannot be achieved without pacifying the mind, helps us to get out of this state of dispersion.

It is clear in the *Discourses* that attention, or *prosochê*, is the foundation needed for the practise of all the spiritual exercises I will detail below. All of them require constant self-awareness of the movement of the mind, assuming full responsibility for our own judgements, actions, desires and fears. Without *prosochê* there can be no *epochê* or *aproptôsia*, which require the mental ability to be mindful at all times.

---

[16] *Discourses* 3.3.20–2 (trans. Hard).

II The Exercises as continual applications of Logic, Physics and Ethics

Despite the loss of treatises by Zeno and Chrysippus, it is possible, with the fragments we have, along with Cicero's, Marcus Aurelius', Seneca's and Epictetus' works to understand the main features of their teaching.

In Stoicism, logic, physics and ethics are not only theoretical disciplines, but also constitute, for students aspiring to live as philosophers, three themes of exercises that must be applied practically.

It appears that there is a certain correspondence between the three parts of the philosophical teaching and the three disciplines as applied by Epictetus in the *Discourses* and the *Handbook* (the focus for these disciplines being *hypolêpsis, orexis* and *hormê*).

For instance, the discipline of desire (*orexis*), which may be understood as *being careful as to the orientation of our desire* when confronting events (Fate), may be perceived as a concrete application of physics. The discipline of impulse (*hormê*) is a part of ethics, and concerns the orientation of our impulse (*hormê*) through the application of the 'duties', which may be positive or negative (duties sometimes to do things, and sometimes to refrain from doing things). And lastly, the discipline of judgement (*hypolêpsis*) is the direct application of logic.

I am now going to describe in detail these different exercises. I do not pretend to offer an exhaustive list, and I have relied heavily on Pierre Hadot's varied research on this subject.[17]

First, I will focus on practical logic, secondly on practical physics, and finally on practical ethics.

A Practical Logic

1 THE DISCIPLINE OF JUDGEMENT

The discipline of judgement is also known as the *proper use of impressions* (sometimes referred to as appearances or representations). Before introducing this major Stoic spiritual exercise, it is well worth studying the concepts of impression (*phantasia*), of

---

[17] Pierre Hadot, *Exercices spirituels et philosophie antique* (Paris: Etudes augustiniennes, 1987).

judgement (*krisis, hypolêpsis*) and of assent (*sunkatathesis*).

Every living being acts in accordance with 'impressions' (*phantasia*) stimulated by the sensible world on the different senses, such that an impression is the '*light in which*' external things or events appear to them. An impression is composed simultaneously or quasi-simultaneously of a perception (that is, an awareness *of something*) which is the cause of a 'first movement of the soul', produced in the *hêgemonikon* (the 'ruling faculty'). This first movement of the soul is the positive (desire/impulsion) or negative (aversion/repulsion) disposition of the *psuchê* toward the thing or event that gave rise to the impression.[18]

---

[18] Note that contemporary research in psychology demonstrates that in the case of stimulus (the sight of an unknown person, say) input from the sensory organs: (1) alerts the thalamus, the sorting centre of incoming information, which then (2) informs the cerebellar tonsils (part of the amygdala in the limbic system), in charge of detecting threats. The cerebellar tonsils (3) activate the hypothalamus, which (4) starts up motor functions for an automatic reaction (running away, attacking, or what have you). In the case of a positive stimuli, another region of the cerebral trunk products dopamine to anticipate a pleasure. The thalamus also alerts the anterior cingulate cortex which (5) focuses attention, leading to the memorisation of emotional experiences. The orbitofrontal cortex is then activated which (6) stimulates emotional areas. The prefrontal cortex is also informed, which (7) analyses the

Consequently, creatures are able to respond to these impressions to search for food, or to take flight from what appears threatening, for example (amongst a wide range of possible actions).

Human beings, just like other creatures, are guided by their sensible impressions. However, because humans have a capacity for reason, we can control our responses with the help of inner discourses (over and above being aware *of something*, human beings also commit to the judgement *that something* is the case, and it is this propositional content of the impression to which someone assents). Thus, when someone engages in such a discourse, they formulate a judgement (*krisis, hupolêpsis, dogma*) that represents the situation as they understand it, and which enables them to assent to the impression. Assent is the movement of the soul which accepts the impression as being *true* by means of this act of judgement. It is thus this *propositional content* of the impression to which human beings assent. Assent is then simultaneously

---

situation to product an emotion. In the span of 500 milliseconds, the first binary information appears: 'I like/I don't like.' This is the emotional shortcut produced by the emotional brain that nobody can control (this is the first movement of the soul). The rational brain reacts afterwards to contextualise the emotion and regulate it (this is the second movement of the soul).

composed of a judgement which itself causes a second movement of the soul, which accepts the impression as being true. The second movement of the soul is then a strengthened positive or negative disposition of the *psuchê* towards the thing or event that produced the impression. It is at this stage that passions (*pathê*[19]) may arise if one's discourse is not conducted properly.

Epictetus gave many examples, both in the *Discourses* and in the *Handbook*.[20] A very famous one concerns a journey by sea:[21] You are on a boat and you can see the sea and the sky, and you can feel the wind. On this occasion, you may assent to this impression by formulating an inner discourse: 'There is some wind,' or 'I can no longer see the harbour.' Judgements such as these may result in a case of mild consternation.

However, other judgements may rise from the subconscious, though not directly stimulated by the reality you have right before your eyes. Therefore, the inner discourse becomes different, and you may say to yourself: 'What a terrible sea!' or 'It will be a

---

[19] The singular term is *pathos*.
[20] See *Handbook* 45, for instance.
[21] *Discourses* 2.16.22.

horrible death!' and a passion such as fear may consequently arise.

Both Marcus and Epictetus draw a clear distinction between 'objective' judgement, which is merely a pure description of reality, and 'subjective' judgement which includes conventional or passionate considerations which have nothing to do with reality. The only way to control our passions is not to give our assent to such subjective impressions.

Pierre Hadot explains that Stoics named some impressions '*phantasia kataleptikê*' or 'comprehensive representation', a representation that is free of any value judgement. This is an objective and primary impression in which no subjective interpretation is present.

The aim of most Stoic spiritual exercises is to resist those subjective judgements that dawn upon what the initial impression implies. Stoics insist on the fact that what is in our power is the correct use of impressions.

2 THE *APROPTÔSIA* OR *EPOCHÊ* EXERCISE

One spiritual exercise that appears regularly in the *Handbook*[22] consists of doubting the initial impression, to wonder whether it is in fact a false one.[23]

This exercise is called *aproptôsia*, and consists of the Stoic practice of not assenting too quickly to judgements that correspond directly to impressions.[24] The concrete application of the discipline of judgement is realised in two steps.

First, the reaction to an impression or inner image which troubles or terrifies us because of its harshness *must be resisted*. This supposes a 'retreat from our projections' which prevent us from seeing 'what is'.

An important element of the ancients' therapy is *epochê*, 'to bracket'; looking at something, somebody, an event and 'to put it in brackets'. We do this in order to 'suspend our judgement', not to project onto the object in question our fears, our desires, and all our 'packets of memories'.

Seeing clearly, primarily is to see what is; what is, and nothing else. *Epochê* concerns emotion as well

---

[22] *Handbook* 3. 4, 9 and 12.
[23] *Discourses* 3.12.15.
[24] *Discourses* 2.8.29.

as judgement and thought. It supposes a great freedom in relation to our reactions. As indicated above, we usually do not control reactive attitudes, which are often mistaken 'actions'. Before even imagining that such a thing is possible, we should be conscious of this. *Epochê* provides a very important moment to allow us to get away from 'our own point of view' and our conditioning before assenting to a *phantasia*. This is the beginning of *clear vision*.

The second step consists of 'adding something' to what the impression initially implies. This second step is called *epilegein* by Epictetus, which means 'saying something more'. The inner discourse, or dialogue with oneself I referred to above, appears at this stage. These mental images give rise to our desires and impulses and are often accompanied by terrifying or alluring value judgements, as I explained above.

The goal of the Stoic *epilegein* is to establish the truth about the impression by distinguishing what is in our power from what is not in our power.[25] Is this thing in your power? If it is in your power, it can be either a good or an evil. If it is not in your power, it is not an evil (though neither can it be a good).

---

[25] *Discourses* 3.3.15; 3.16.15.

Epictetus imagines that impressions ask us questions,[26] and that is why the *epilegein* is a form of inner dialogue.

It is important to remember that our *hêgemonikon* is constantly stimulated by impressions. A regular meditative practice, as detailed in the last part of this essay, is of great help, for it aims at developing attention and pacifying the mind.

We will now investigate how the spiritual exercises apply to Stoic physics and ethics.

B   Practical Physics

1   The Discipline of Desire (and aversion)

How should we define the discipline of desire?

Epictetus advises those wishing to practise this discipline to bear insults,[27] to drink wine with moderation, to refrain from eating a cake or having sex with a beautiful girl, not to be afraid of poverty, illness or death, or again, not to pursue honour or riches.

Desires correspond to the attraction we have to-

---

[26] *Discourses* 3.8.1–6.
[27] *Discourses* 3.12.10.

wards what we believe is good and of which we can be deprived, and aversions correspond to the repulsion we feel towards what we believe is evil, and consequently fear.

Thus, the discipline of desire is concerned first, with things that affect us, and secondly, with the search for a certain state of mind by reaching for a good or avoiding an evil.

It seems that for many philosophers, the simple act of desire is in itself a sickness, a sign of dissatisfaction, a more or less painful 'deficiency'.

In the *Handbook*, Epictetus insists on the fact that his students should stop having desires. This seems surprising. One may perfectly understand that Epictetus forbids the desire for things which are not 'up to us', 'because we might loose them and as a consequence fall prey to a 'passion'. But how could it not be right to desire things which are 'up to us' and which conform to nature? How could it be possible not to desire moral goodness, being capable of right judgement and right action, that is, to desire *eudaimonia*?

In fact, evil does not lie in the act of desiring, for it is a sign of life, *but in the bad orientation of desire*. Intrinsic to the drama of human life is the desire that people have for external goods; but although external goods are in fact transitory, people often mistake them for having a reality they do not have, believing them to be unchanging.

The perversion of desire is to idolise objects. When someone fails to reach their goal, another state of mind arises such as the passion of sadness, fear or anger. For this reason, Epictetus also calls the discipline of desire, the discipline of the passions.[28]

Epictetus wishes to teach us to take care of our desire, to reorient the desire towards virtue. The reason why he recommends that we stop having desires is simple.

Here we should recognise one of the most powerful ancient spiritual practices (later adopted by the Christians): you should not pretend that you can immediately reach a high state of perfection without ascetic preparation. You should start by developing an aversion to your own irrational behaviour, and learn to identify your flaws. Desiring an inaccessible perfection before 'cleansing your soul' runs the risk of creating sadness and discouragement.

2   EXAMPLES OF *EPILEGEIN* IN DESIRE

a. Praemeditation malorum. It is not enough to agree to *accept* events once they have happened, a

---

[28] *Discourses* 3.2.3.

Stoic student should learn to anticipate such events.

One of the most important Stoic exercises is that of the *praemeditatio*, in which Stoic students prepare themselves to endure unpleasant or painful experiences.

It consists in representing to oneself anything which may occur in the course of daily life: difficulties, setbacks, sufferings or even death, for instance. Of course, practising the *praemeditatio*, the Stoic wishes to smooth the impact of unpleasant events (but not to escape from them) and above all to restore his peace of mind.

Marcus Aurelius, for example, used to practise premeditation in the morning, trying to foresee difficult issues in dealing with people:

> Say to yourself at break of day, I shall meet with meddling, ungrateful, violent, treacherous, envious and ungrateful men. All these vices have fallen to them because they have no knowledge of good and bad. But I, who have beheld the nature of the good, and seen what is the right; and of the bad, and seen that it is the wrong; and of the wrongdoer himself, and seeing that his nature is akin to my own—not because he is of the same blood and seed, but because he shares with me in mind and a portion of the divine—I, then, can never be harmed by any of these men, nor can I

become angry with one who is akin to me, nor can I hate him, for we have come into being to work together, like feet, hands, or eyelids, or the two rows of teeth in our upper and lower jaws. To work against one another is therefore contrary to nature; and to be angry with another and turn away from him is surely to work against him.[29]

In fact, we should not be afraid to entertain in our thoughts the sort of thing that other people consider to be evil. To be sure, we should think about these things often, to remind ourselves, first that future evils are not evils because they are not yet present, and secondly that events such as disease, poverty and death are not evils because they are not in our power, and consequently have no bearing on morality.

One important thing to note is that the constant thought of death radically transforms our way of living, for it makes us realise the sheer value of every single moment of time:

> At every hour devote yourself in a resolute spirit, as suits a Roman and a man, to fulfilling the task in hand with scrupulous and unaffected dignity, and

---

[29] *Meditations* 2.1 (trans. Hard).

love for others, and independence and justice; and grant yourself a respite from all other preoccupations. And this you will achieve if you perform every action as though it were your last, freed from all lack of purpose and wilful deviation from the rule of reason, and from duplicity, self-seeking, and dissatisfaction with what is allotted to you.[30]

This exercise is intimately linked to the discipline of desire, because when a Stoic acts he foresees every obstacle, and consequently nothing really happens against his will, and his purity of intention remains unchanged.

Deepening your understanding

Praemeditation is indeed not an easy exercise; sometimes it may lead to serious misunderstanding.

The idea is that generally, we act in accordance with our expectations. If we expect everything to be easy and agreeable then, when the first problem arises, we will be discouraged. But if, on the contrary, we are

---

[30] *Meditations* 2.5 (trans. Hard).

prepared for things to be disagreeable, if we anticipate great difficulties and many formidable obstacles, we need never be discouraged as we strive to make progress in our undertakings.

Having adopted this new outlook, difficulties will in consequence appear very minor, because we were expecting worse ones. This perspective may be applied to many different cases. Generally speaking, we tend to hope for too much. We wish for our lives to be agreeable and easy, and we expect too much from other people; consequently, many problems arise. But, if we do not have any particular expectations, every single positive event can make us happy — a kindly word from someone, for example, that pleasantly surprises us.

This exercise is of great help in developing a virtue such as courage (*andreia*, confidence, strength of mind and magnanimity — what we might today call perseverance). It also teaches us to live and appreciate the present moment, to enjoy what we presently have, and also to fully understand the notion of impermanence.

However, some people have great difficulty practising this exercise. For example, they cannot imagine the death of their child without feeling troubled, and they start imagining many distressing things, and thus open themselves to a passion associated with fear. This, of course, is not the aim of the exercise.

Those who experience this difficulty are evidently not yet ready for this kind of exercise, and for the time being it will be better that they put it aside.

b. Physical Definition. This exercise is a typical example of *epilegein*. It consists of defining in precise terms what it is that one is attached to, and therefore wishes to hold on to. The definition will enable us to distinguish clearly subjective and affective judgements from the objective representation that we should have concerning the things to which we are attached.

Thus, Marcus Aurelius says:

Always define or describe whatever presents itself to your mind, so as to see what sort of thing it is when stripped to its essence, as a whole and in its separate parts; and tell yourself its proper name, and the names of the elements from which it was compounded and into which it will finally be resolved.[31]

The discipline of desire implies successfully reducing desire for material possessions or social position. Consequently, this exercise must apply to everything that surrounds us, and we must try to see these things as they truly are. Try to apply it when you wander down streets lined with enticing shops: I can assure you that it works!

Epictetus himself used to recommend to his students the practice of this exercise:

> In the case of particular things that delight you, or benefit you, or to which you have grown attached, remind yourself of what they are. Start with things of little value. If it is china you like, for instance, say, 'I am fond of a piece of china.' When it breaks, then you won't be as disconcerted. When giving your wife or child a kiss, repeat to yourself, 'I am kissing a mor-

---

[31] *Meditations* 3.11 (trans. Hard).

tal.' Then you won't be so distraught if they are taken from you.[32]

The same method is to be applied to people who think themselves important:

> Imagine them as they are when they are eating, when they are sleeping, when they are making love, or going to the bathroom. Then imagine them when they are putting on airs; when they make those haughty gestures, or when they get angry and upbraid people with such a superior air.[33]

Of course, the goal of this exercise is to acquire an inner detachment from the things around us, including the things we love (but also the things we are afraid of), and it has to be practised progressively. As you begin to detach yourself from external things, you may have a new sense of being separated from everything and, in being separated, you will experience a new sense of freedom, but also, to be sure, you may develop a new awareness of your own mortality.

---

[32] Arrian's *Handbook* of Epictetus, Chapter 3, trans. Robert Dobbin, *Epictetus Discourses and Selected Writings* (London: Penguin, 2008), 222.

[33] *Meditations* 9.9 (trans. Hadot, *The Inner Citadel*, 165).

c. Restitution. One of the core teachings of Stoicism is understanding that everything you possess (riches, honours, as well as the people you love) may be taken from you at any time.

Epictetus explained:

> Under no circumstances ever say 'I have lost something,' only 'I returned it.' Did a child of yours die? No, it was returned. Your wife died? No, *she* was returned. 'My land was confiscated.' No, it too was returned.
>
> 'But the person who took it was a thief.'
>
> Why concern yourself with the means by which the original giver effects its return? As long as he entrusts it to you, look after it as something yours to enjoy only for a time—the way a traveller regards a hotel.[34]

Consequently, the Stoic outlook on these things is always to see them as being mere loans, because a loan must always be returned to its true owner one day or another. So when you are about to lose your life or some possession, or when you learn that a person that you cherished has died and you feel sad,

---

[34] *Handbook* 11 (trans. Dobbin).

the following sentence should immediately come to mind: *it is a restitution*.

To sum up, we should get used to the idea that we will lose everything that we love: as you may guess, this little exercise is designed to instil detachment from everything that for the non-philosopher is supposed to have value, and is ultimately a means to reach inner freedom.[35]

d. Impermanence or universal metamorphosis. Ancient Stoics linked ethics and the good life to a full comprehension of Nature, and consequently a form of meditation has been designed to educate the Stoic student in the comprehension of impermanence, and to appreciate the link which binds all living beings on this earth.

Ultimately, this enables us to understand what our place is in this constantly ever-changing universe. In this sense, Stoicism is undoubtedly a spiritual path, for it develops in students a deep love for the world which created them and everything which surrounds them.

Comprehension of impermanence can be achieved by various means: by way of the writing meditation, or by way of an *epilegein*. It is possible,

---

[35] *Discourses* 1.1.32 and 1.24.14.

but there is no evidence at all, that these practices included visualisation techniques. Reconstruction of these types of exercise will require much imagination and meditative practical knowledge from us. This will take some time I am afraid, but it is necessary, for I believe Stoicism will remain incomplete without this aspect of the philosophy.

A good example of applied physics is the exercise called 'universal metamorphosis'. In this exercise the Stoic trains themselves to observe how things constantly change.

Marcus Aurelius describes it in this way:

> Acquire a method to examine systematically how all things are transformed from one to another, and direct your attention constantly to this area of study, and exercise yourself in it, for nothing is so conducive to elevation of mind.[36]

And again:

> Look carefully at every existing thing and reflect that its dissolution is already under way and it is in the

---

[36] *Meditations* 10.11 (trans. Hard).

course of change and, as it were, of decay or dispersal, or is dying in whatever way its nature appoints.[37]

In this case, this meditation could involve visualisation techniques. For instance, you may try to visualise a tree, and try to follow its evolution through the seasons. Or again, you can visualise a human body through the stages of life, then its death and decay.

In fact, a large variety of objects are suitable subjects for this meditation. Finding appropriate subjects for the 'universal metamorphosis' exercise could contribute to its effectiveness for the Stoic apprentice.

e. *Wand of Hermes*. The 'Wand of Hermes' exercise is another way of not being overwhelmed by one's impressions. When something 'bad' happens to you, you should immediately distinguish what is up to you from what is not up to you.

This traditional distinction is so important that it is the subject of the opening chapter of Epictetus' *Handbook*:

---

[37] *Meditations* 10.18 (trans. Hard).

We are responsible for some things, while there are others for which we cannot be held responsible. The former include our judgement, our impulse, our desire, aversion and our mental faculties in general; the latter include the body, material possessions, our reputation, status—in a word, anything not in our power to control. The former are naturally free, unconstrained and unimpeded, while the latter are frail, inferior, subject to restraint—and none of our affair.[38]

Epictetus refers to this exercise in a whole discourse:[39] our *hêgemonikon* finds in every occasion the ability and the opportunity to exercise virtue by way of correct judgement.

In fact, it is like the wand of Hermes, which has the power to change everything to gold.

> No one calls 'good' the fact that it is day, or 'bad' that it is night, or 'the greatest of evils' that three is equal to four. No, they call correct judgement good and incorrect judgement bad—the consequence being that good even comes of error, when we recognize the error as such.
>
> And so it should be in life. 'Being healthy is good,

---

[38] *Handbook* 1 (trans. Robert Dobbin).
[39] *Discourses* 3.20.

being sick is bad.' No, my friend: enjoying health in the right way is good; making bad use of your health is bad. 'So even illness can benefit us?' Why not, if even death and disability can?[40]

The one who insults you gives you the occasion to exercise patience. Illness gives you the occasion to exercise courage and serenity. Death obliges you to conform your will to Nature's own will. Other examples of duties are, as Epictetus would say 'eat as a man, drink as a man, clean yourself as a man, marry, have children, lead the proper life of a citizen, and so forth.'[41]

Stoicism is, I think, a very realistic but optimistic philosophy: life may not be easy, but it is up to you to see things differently and to obtain strength from developing this new outlook on life.

f. Self-expansion into the world. This exercise, an exercise of imagination or probably visualization, is not an easy one to practise.

It was first of all recommended by Plato and consists in a kind of 'dilation' of the self into the totality

---

[40] Arrian's *Discourses* of Epictetus, 3.20.2–5, trans. Robert Dobbin, *Epictetus Discourses and Selected Writings* (London: Penguin, 2008), 155.
[41] See for instance *Discourses* 2.23.38, 3.1.44; *Handbook* 46.

of the real. The soul 'strives to ceaselessly embrace the whole universality of the divine and the human' and towards 'the contemplation of the whole of time and of being'. Thus the soul rises into the heights and governs the whole world, while our body remains where it is.[42]

In the Stoic tradition, any one individual soul is but a tiny spark of the world soul. So, for Stoics, this exercise consists in letting the 'self' or 'soul' plunge into the totality of the world, and feel with joy its closeness with the *logos* which governs everything from inside.

Seneca describes this exercise to Lucilius,[43] but Marcus Aurelius does the same in some of his *Meditations*:

> [The rational soul] traverses the whole universe and the void which encircles it and surveys its form, and reaches out into the endlessness of infinite time, and comprehends and reflects upon the periodic rebirth of the whole, and perceives that those who will come after us will see nothing new, just as those who came before us saw nothing more, but that in a sense of a

---

[42] See for instance, Plato, *Thaeatetus* 173c, *Republic* 486a; Pierre Hadot, 'The View from Above', in *Philosophy as a Way of Life* (Oxford: Blackwell 1995), 238–50.
[43] See Seneca, *Moral Letters* 102.21.

forty-year-old, if he has a modicum of understanding, has seen all that has been and all that ever will be because it is ever the same.[44]

And:

Watch the stars in their courses as though you were accompanying them on their way, and reflect perpetually on how the elements are constantly changing from one to another; for the thought of these things purifies us from the defilement of our earthly existence.[45]

Also:

Continually picture to yourself the whole of time and the whole of substance, and reflect that any particular part of them, when measured against substance overall is but a fig-seed, and when measured against time, but the single turn of a drill.[46]

As Pierre Hadot remarks,[47] this exercise, in the

---

[44] *Meditations* 11.1 (trans. Hard).
[45] *Meditations* 7.47 (trans. Hard).
[46] *Meditations* 10.17 (trans. Hard).
[47] Pierre Hadot, *What is Ancient Philosophy?* (Cambridge, MA: Belknap Press of Harvard University Press, 2002), 202–6.

second quotation above, pictures the philosopher focusing his awareness on his being as located within the All, as a minuscule point of duration, but capable nevertheless of merging into the immensity of infinite space and of seizing the whole of reality in a single intuition.

This is also the occasion to remind ourselves how brief the time is that we have been granted when compared with the long history of the cosmos, and consequently how important our daily practice is.

g. The view from above. Some Stoics I know are very fond of this exercise.[48]

The 'view from above' exercise consists in looking at things with detachment, distance, and objectivity, as if you were seeing the Earth from space, or from the Moon.

From there, consider the luxuries of the wealthy

---

[48] Ronald Robertson, author of *The Philosophy of Cognitive Behavioural Therapy: Stoic Philosophy as Rational and Cognitive Psychotherapy* (London: Karnac Books, 2010), offers in Appendix II a transcript of the 'View from above exercise' that he has used with many hundreds of people. He states that he and his colleagues have been surprised by how much people seem to enjoy and feel a sense of benefit from merely listening to the transcript. They have also found it useful to provide people with recordings of this transcript on CD or MP3. (Donald Robertson's transcript also includes the element 'Self-expansion into the world'.)

and the rich gloating over their possessions; the borders which people erect between each other should appear ridiculous; armies invading territories should look like ants fighting over a narrow space, and so forth.

This exercise is a good one to learn for situating things within the immensity of the Universe and the totality of Nature, without the false prestige lent to them by our human passions and conventions.

Marcus Aurelius wrote:

> Crowds, armies, farmers; weddings, divorces, births, deaths; the hubbub of the courts; deserted places; the diversity of the customs of barbarous peoples; celebrations, lamentations; marketplaces: what a hodgepodge! And yet there is the harmony of contraries.[49]

The 'view from above' should change our judgement on things concerning luxury, power, war, borders and the worries of everyday life, whether these occur within our families, at work or elsewhere, by resituating them within the immensity of the cosmos and the vastness of human experience.

Indeed, when we look at things from the perspective of the Cosmos, those things which do not

---

[49] *Meditations* 7.48 (trans. Hadot, *The Inner Citadel*, 173).

depend on us, and which Stoics call 'indifferents', are brought back to their true proportions.

> Short is the time which each of us lives; puny the little corner of earth on which we live; how puny, finally, is even the lengthiest posthumous glory. Even this glory, moreover, is transmitted by little men who'll soon be dead, without even having known themselves, much less him who has long since been dead.[50]

This exercise, then, should also help us contemplate how foolish most of our actions are, and remind us of the imminence of death ... and the urgency of our practice!

C Practical Ethics

1 THE DISCIPLINE OF IMPULSE

The discipline of impulse engages our sense of responsibility. It addresses how we relate to other human beings, those of our kind who may be the source of passions *because* they are of our kind and

---

[50] *Meditations* 3.10.2 (trans. Hadot, *The Inner Citadel*, 175).

because we should care for them, despite the fact that on occasion they may be despicable.

The discipline of impulse is of course linked to the discipline of desire, for a person not subject to passions is more likely to act wisely, that is, to act in a way appropriate to nature.

This idea is rendered in Stoic philosophy by the very important notion of *kathêkon*. A *kathêkon*—often translated in English as duty—represents for Stoics an action appropriate to nature. Such actions, which are up to us, also suppose an intention to do something (or not do something, or prevent something) that cannot be accomplished with an indifferent disposition. We should note and avoid a potential misunderstanding: these actions concern items and situations that are technically referred to as 'indifferent' (that is, neither good nor bad). In these cases, what happens is not entirely 'up to us', but rather up to other people, circumstances or external events.

In order to design a practical code of conduct by means of which we may select from among the indifferent things, any of which may be the objects of our actions, Stoics noticed, as a starting point, that a fundamental instinct of nature was an expression of the 'will' of Nature.

Indeed, thanks to a natural impulse, every being

on earth has an appropriate regard for themselves, such that they select what is most suited for their survival and avoid what may be a threat to their well-being. Through this natural instinct, that which is appropriate to nature is revealed.

According to Stoic philosophy, this natural impulse should be exerted with respect to the hierarchy introduced by nature's *scala naturae*. Stoics have indeed developed a very interesting theory about nature's inner levels (*scala naturae*) and divided the universe into four levels: *hexis* (stones), *phusis* (flowers, plants, trees), *psuchê* (animals) and finally *nous* (a characteristic belonging only to human beings). Human beings, the most complex creation of Nature, are composed of all four of these levels, and in relation to impulse a number of consequences follow.

For example, the word '*phusis*' also means 'strength or growth', and human beings, like plants, also possess this capacity which directs them, for instance, to feed themselves, to clothe themselves, and to breed. This capacity concerns in essence the taking care of one's body.

But human beings not only possess a 'capacity for growth', but also a 'capacity for sensation' (*psuchê*): this is a higher level of capacity, which is also called the 'capacity of the animal'. Human beings, like animals, are free to move and act according to their impressions, whether these impressions originate from sensory perception or in the mind as something imagined or thought about. Above all, human beings are animals living in communities, a feature essential for their survival. And this being the case, self-preservation is achieved through the vigilance of the senses. It is interesting to note that the terms '*psuchê*' (soul) and '*pneuma*' (breath) have the same etymological origin: indeed, the Stoics thought that 'intelligent' *pneuma* extending throughout the human body was the medium for sensation (*aisthêsis*). *Pneuma* may be then considered as the gateway to the *psuchê*. Thus self-preservation is taking care of your *psuchê*.

However, if exaggerated, the role of sensation could have a bad influence on an even higher level of capacity called '*nous*' or '*hêgemonikon*', that which enables human beings to consent to the great laws of Nature, or to fate, and to the events that are parts of this universal nature.

I will describe below some exercises that are usually linked to this discipline.

2 Examples of *Epilegein* in Impulse

The discipline of action should be added to the rigorous discipline of desire, but should be practised with measure and reservation.

a. Defining the planned action. Epictetus, in Chapter 4 of the *Handbook*, talks about activities we are planning to undertake. It is important that we remind ourselves of every turn of event that may possibly occur as a result of attempting to complete our activity.

> When you are going to take in hand any act, remind yourself what kind of an act it is. If you are going to bathe, place before yourself what happens in the bath: some splashing the water, others pushing against one another, others abusing one another, and some stealing; and thus with more safety you will undertake the matter, if you say to yourself, I now intend to bathe, and to maintain my will in a manner conformable to nature. And so you will do in every act: for thus if any hindrance to bathing shall happen, let this thought be ready; it was not this only that I intended, but I intended also to maintain my will in a way

conformable to nature; but I shall not maintain it so, if I am vexed at what happens (trans. Long).

Bathing is ordinarily considered to be a very agreeable activity, but it can also be accompanied with several possible misfortunes. Seneca had already used the example of bathing to illustrate the exercise of premeditation applied to the discipline of action.[51] This exercise is also linked to the practice of 'acting with reservation' described below.

This exercise helps the Stoic *prokoptôn* to never forget that the most important thing is to ensure the purity of their intention.

A very important notion should be introduced here. As in any other art or profession, the 'job' of being a Stoic philosopher has its own goal (*skopos*) and end (*telos*). *Telos* in this sense means '*reward*', and *skopos* means '*running in the stadium*'.

The *telos* of the Stoic philosopher, his reward, is of course *eudaimonia*, which Zeno defined as being a 'good flow of life'. But *eudaimonia* is often both a concept difficult to grasp and something that many of us may well find far removed from our day-to-day preoccupations, and the preserve of the Sage only.

---

[51] *Epistulae Morales ad Lucilium* 107.2.

That is why the philosopher needs something to serve as a benchmark, a *skopos*, that will indicate whether or not they are still behaving in the right way. *Skopos* is defined as being the will of the *psuchê*, a constant application of the mind from which the Stoic philosopher should never depart.[52]

The *skopos* of the Stoic philosopher, as Musonius Rufus would have said, is being attentive to *the purity of intention*. This purity of intention is then the sole guide or reference for the philosopher's desires and actions. In order to ensure this purity of intention, the Stoic student has to be well disciplined; they must submit themselves to training for making proper use of impressions, to a diet, to reading, and to practising the virtues.

Ancient Greek is very clear when it says '*kata skopon diôkô*' or '*I am running, guiding myself to the goal*'. If the Stoic forgets to stick to their goal with strength and perseverance, they will be then unable to reach their *telos*, the eudaimonistic life.

---

[52] See a very interesting collation of St John Cassian where Abba Moise explains in details the doctrine of *telos* and *skopos* within the framework of early Christian philosophy. I chose to adopt this interpretation, as I believe that it helps to understand better the ancient Stoic sources, and was probably inspired by them, than the usual explanation given by scholars who link these notions with the uncertainty of the outcome of our actions.

Ancient Stoics used the analogy of the archer shooting at a target to explain this notion:

> Take the case of one whose task it is to shoot a spear or arrow straight at some target [*skopos*]. One's ultimate aim [*telos*] is to do all in one's power to shoot straight, and the same applies with our ultimate good. In this kind of example, it is to shoot straight that one must do all one can; none the less, it is to do all one can to accomplish the task that is really the ultimate aim. It is just the same with what we call the supreme good in life. To actually hit the target is, as we say, to be selected but not sought.[53]

Chapter 4 of the *Handbook* quoted above, underlines the fact that the *prokoptôn* should always remember that they *now intend to bathe (or any other action), and to maintain their will in a manner conformable to nature*. In this way, they should never forget 'to run, guiding themselves to the goal'.

b. Acting 'with reservation'. 'Acting with reservation' is a technical expression: someone acts with

---

[53] Cicero, *On Ends* 3.22, trans. Raphael Woolf, *Cicero: On Moral Ends*, ed. Julia Annas (Cambridge: Cambridge University Press, 2001), 72.

reservation when they realise that in attempting to fulfil their action it is entirely possible that they will meet with obstacles that are independent of their will, and that may well prevent success.

The Stoic foresees (or tries to foresee) every obstacle, and so keeps their equanimity in all circumstances, because this will help them to remain faithful to the way of life they have chosen.

Seneca says:

> The wise man sets about every action with reservation: 'if nothing happens which might stop him'. For this reason, we say that he always succeeds and that nothing unexpected happens to him: because within himself he considers the possibility that something will get in the way and prevent what he is proposing to do.[54]

And again:

> The safest policy is rarely to tempt [Fortune], though to keep her always in mind and to trust her in nothing. Thus: 'I shall sail unless something happens'; and

---

[54] *On Benefits* 4.34.4, trans Donini, Inwood and Donini in Keimpe Algra, et al. (eds.) *The Cambridge History of Hellenistic Philosophy* (Cambridge: Cambridge University Press, 1999), 737.

'I shall become praetor unless something prevents me', and 'My business will be successful unless something interferes'. That is why we say that nothing happens to a wise man against his expectations.[55]

Regarding this exercise, Keith Seddon explains that

Once we realise that things that happen in the world, including the way other people act, are not wholly in our power, we come into possession of a wonderful gift, for now we can engage in our affairs with a sort of serenity, a new found peace of mind and an empowering confidence.[56]

However, these exercises, that are variations of premeditation, are not easy to practise.

Marcus Aurelius warns us:

Do not disturb yourself by picturing your life as a whole; do not assemble in your mind the many and

---

[55] *On Tranquility of Mind* 13.2–3, trans. Costa in C. D. N. Costa, *Seneca: Dialogues and Letters* (London: Penguin, 1997), 51–2.

[56] Keith Seddon, *Stoic Serenity: A Practical Course on Finding Inner Peace* (Morrisville, NC: Lulu, 2006), 43.

varied troubles which have come to you in the past and will come again in the future.[57]

The answer to this problem is to concentrate not only on present actions, but also on present difficulties, which then become an easier burden to bear, as they are confined to the present moment only. It is very important not to fall prey *in the present* to some *future* anguish.

c. Acting for the good of the community. The discipline of action consists essentially in acting for the good of the community. I will not rehearse here the theoretical foundation that explains why, according to Stoic philosophy, Universal Nature has made rational beings for the sake of one another. I will only stress the practical consequences of this statement, because this is often the most problematic in daily practice.

There is a great Socratic tradition, of which Epictetus thought it important to remind his students from time to time, according which *No one is voluntarily evil.* According to Stoic philosophy, human beings naturally desire the good, and spontaneously tend towards that which seems to them to

---

[57] *Meditations* 8.36 (trans. Hard).

be good. If a burglary has been committed, it is because the thief was absolutely convinced that stealing the possessions of other people was a 'good' for him; and in doing so, he was deceived by his impression of where the good lay, but he did not for all that desire evil for evil's sake.

Nevertheless, in confronting the thief's action, the difficulty we now have consists in how we may remain benevolent towards him. Epictetus describes the ideal Stoic attitude:

> With regard to those who are different from him [by the principles of their life], he will be patient, gentle, delicate, and forgiving, as he would toward someone in a state of ignorance, who missed the mark when it came to the most important things. He will not be harsh to anyone, for he will have perfectly understood Plato's words: 'Every soul is deprived of the truth against its will.'[58]

This attitude, that Marcus and Epictetus call 'pity'—though of course not referring to the passion in this case—is first a state of lack of anger and hatred towards those who behave badly. However, above all, it is also the will to help them by inform-

---

[58] *Discourses* 2.22.36 (trans. Hadot, *The Inner Citadel*, 224).

ing them about their error, and teaching them genuine values to help them to be *eudaimôn*, and thus removing all traces of suffering.

This attitude is close to what the Buddhists calls in Sanskrit *Karuna*, and which is poorly translated in English by the term 'compassion'. Buddhists describe several levels of compassion according to the degree of the individual's comprehension and realisation. The highest form of compassion is the one that accompanies total comprehension and perfect understanding of the nature of things. We realise that all the beings who suffer so much do not need to suffer. Suffering is simply the consequence of confusion, an erroneous way of seeing and thinking. If they could see things differently, they could be free of suffering. Compassion becomes very powerful when we clearly see that suffering, while so common, is in fact so easy to remove. What prevents beings from attaining liberation (= *eudaimonia?*) is in fact a thin veil, and yet, through ignorance, beings are suffering intensely and in a totally pointless way.

Buddhists of the Tibetan tradition have established a powerful tool to develop this attitude of benevolence, which is called *Tonglen*. However, this training should only be undertaken when the basic meditative practice of Samatha-Vipassyana is well known and understood.

I will not expand upon Tonglen here, for it does not belong to Stoic tradition, though it is perhaps worth remarking that the Stoic may well be interested in looking into this training. Indeed, although the outlooks that both the Stoic and Buddhist traditions recommend seem to be very close, I have not noted any traces of an *askêsis* belonging to the ancient Greek tradition that can be interpreted as being designed for developing compassion. Only the Christian Hesychastic Prayer could be seen as a notable exception.

d. Acting according to value (kat' axian). Another characteristic of the goodness of impulse is that impulses must be in accordance with value (*kat'axian*).
Marcus Aurelius said:

> I see all things as they are, and I use each of them in accordance with its value (*kat' axian*).[59]

The Stoics had long since developed a rather elaborate theory of value that Diogenes Laertius summarises thus:

---

[59] *Meditations* 8.29 (trans. Hadot, *The Inner Citadel*, 216).

And they say that to benefit is to change or sustain something according to virtue; whereas to harm is to change or sustain something according to vice.

They also assert that things indifferent are so spoken of in two different ways; firstly, those things are called so, which have no influence in producing either happiness or unhappiness, such as, for instance, riches, glory, health, strength, and the like; for it is possible for someone to be happy without any of these things; and also, it is upon the character of the use that is made of them that happiness or unhappiness depends. In another sense, those things are called indifferent which do not excite any impulse towards or aversion away from something, such as, for instance, the fact of someone's having an odd or an even number of hairs on their head, or someone's putting out or drawing back their finger; for it is not in this sense that the things previously mentioned are called indifferent, for they do excite impulse or aversion. On which account some of them are selected and some rejected, though there is no reason for choosing or shunning all the others.

Again, of things indifferent, they call some preferred, and others rejected. Preferred are those which have value, and rejected are those which have no value at all. And by the term value, they mean that quality of things which causes them to contribute to producing a well-regulated life; and in this sense, every good has value. Again, they say that a thing has value when from some point of view it has a sort of intermediate potential or usefulness which contributes to a life in accordance with nature; and under this class we may arrange riches or good health if they give any assistance to living in accordance with nature. Again, value is accorded to the price which one gives to acquire an object, and is fixed as its fair price by someone who has experience of the object sought, as occurs for instance when some wheat is to be exchanged for barley, along with a mule thrown in to make up the difference.[60]

Stoics thus distinguished three degrees of value:

(1) the Good has supreme value because it contributes to producing a well-regulated life;

(2) the indifferents have 'value' when from some point of view they have a sort of potential or usefulness which contributes to a life in accordance with nature: food, shelter, health, a job by means of which one may earn one's living, and so forth;

---

[60] Diogenes Laertius 7.104–5, trans. C. D. Yonge and Keith Seddon, *A Summary of Stoic Philosophy: Zeno of Citium in Diogenes Laertius Book Seven* (Morrisville, NC: Lulu 2007), 76–77.

(3) the third meaning of 'value' is value accorded to the price which one gives to acquire an object.

To recognise the exact value of a thing is thus a very important exercise, which is part of the discipline of judgement. This helps to regulate the impulse to action and distribute the intensity of our actions proportionately to value.

Seneca had defined the discipline of action as follows: we should in the first place, judge the value of the matter in question, then adjust our impulse to act according to this value and, finally we should bring impulse and action into harmony, so that we always remain in accord with ourselves.

The difficulty with acting in accordance with value following Stoic teaching, is that the Stoics do not have the same scale of value that other people have. This can be problematic for the beginner, who is liable to be carried away and value things according to the standards that ordinary people usually apply in daily life. However, it is possible, as I shall now attempt to show, to test our ability and motivation in order to continue on the Stoic path.

III Attempt to reconstruct a Stoic meditation

A The help of Buddhist Samatha-Vipassyana therapy

Having found a very interesting quotation in Epictetus' *Discourses*, I am convinced that the ancient Stoics had their own system of meditation:

> The soul is like a vessel filled with water; and impressions are like a ray of light that falls upon the water. If the water is disturbed, the ray will seem to be disturbed likewise, though in reality it is not. Whenever, therefore, a man is seized with vertigo, it is not the arts and virtues that are confounded, but the spirit in which they exist; and, if this comes to rest, so will they likewise.[61]

At first sight, it appeared to me that Epictetus describes a typical meditation technique which seems

---

[61] *Discourses* 3.3.20-2 (trans. Hard).

to be similar in many respects to the Buddhist's Samatha-Vipassyana. This basic Buddhist meditation technique[62] is seen as a process in which one aims to re-educate one's mind. The state one wishes to reach is one in which one is fully conscious of everything that happens in one's immediate experience, exactly in the way that it happens, exactly when it happens with a total consciousness of the present moment.

To accomplish this, the Buddhists teach a technique to pacify the mind, which is called 'Samatha': to be sure that their students will understand the goal of meditation, they often compare the mind to a pool of water, very similar to the way Epictetus' does in his analogy, which I find really striking.

In his *Discourses*, Epictetus refers only to the contemplation of impressions. In fact, it appears that our whole mind is 'made up' of impressions reflected by our mind 'like a sunray that falls upon the water'. Consequently, we should be able to observe them carefully.

> For what purpose, then, have we received reason from nature? To make a proper use of impressions.

---

[62] In Henepola Gunaratama, *Mindfulness in Plain English* (Somerville, MA: Wisdom Publications, 1992).

And what is reason itself? Something compounded from impressions of a certain kind: and, thus, by its nature, it becomes contemplative of itself too.[63]

It is consequently plausible to think that the Stoics taught the pacification of mind in their meditation system because such a contemplative work would really be impossible without active attention.

After having pacified the mind, the Buddhist progressively learns to observe all phenomena (thoughts, emotions, physical sensations) which arise in the mind: this is the 'vipassyana' component of their meditative system. It is the capacity to have an awareness of something without being captivated by it.

For example, it means being aware of a thought without thinking the thought. Or again 'seeing' a thought, emotion or sensation as one would observe a car passing on a motorway, for instance. I suspect that this describes a capacity of the *hêgemonikon* as the ancient Stoics understood it.

The importance of *prosochê*, but also the practice of *epochê*, confirmed for me some years ago that ancient philosophers in general, and Stoics in particular, would have had a method for teaching their

---

[63] *Discourses* 1.20.5 (trans. Hard).

followers a way to internalise this capacity, that essentially parallels basic Buddhist meditative technique.

However, I found that my interpretation of this matter was so alien to modern scholars, and even to most contemporary Stoics, that I wanted to work on this further, to improve my own meditative practice before trying to present a more clearly worked out exposition. 'Revelation', I dare say, came when I began to read early Christian literature.

B   The help of the Hesychastic Prayer tradition

I discovered some years ago that early Christians were sometimes deeply inspired by ancient philosophers, and especially the Stoics, to cultivate their own therapy. A good example may be found in the works of Jean-Yves Leloup, an orthodox theologian, who is well known in France as a popular author on spirituality and psychology (indeed, many of his books are now available in English translation).

Having studied with the Athos monks, he shared with us (in *Being still, Reflections on an Ancient*

Mystical Tradition[64]) the way of Hesychastic prayer according to Father Seraphin.

This teaching is a purely natural and therapeutic way of meditating, using the *scala naturae* (*hexis, phusis, psuchê, nous*). Humanity has indeed often lost contact with these natural elements, which go together to form our microcosm, and this often leads to all sorts of discomfort, sickness, insecurity and anxiety. The individual feels unwelcome, estranged from the world. That is why meditation, according to the ancients, has as its first task, entering into contemplation and praise of the entire universe.

In my attempt to reconstruct a probable original Stoic *askêsis/meletê*, I tried to isolate from this orthodox teaching the philosophical elements that early Christians obviously borrowed from the Stoics. This adaptation is only a taster, as any exercise of this sort should not be transmitted without the help of a qualified instructor.

It is important to stress the prominence of the oral transmission. It is very probable that if such an exercise really existed within the ancient Stoic tradition, its transmission would have been effected

---

[64] Jean-Yves Leloup, *Being Still, Reflections on an Ancient Mystical Tradition*, translated and edited by M. S. Laird (Gracewing/Paulist Press, 2003).

exclusively by way of oral teaching. This would explain why it is now impossible to find any written descriptions in the extant literature.

1 TO MEDITATE LIKE A MOUNTAIN (*HEXIS*)

The first instructions concerns stability: settling into a good posture. Indeed, the first counsel to give anyone who wants to meditate is not on the spiritual level, but on the physical. Sit down.

'To sit like a mountain also means to feel your weight, to be heavy with presence.'[65] At the beginning, you may find it difficult remaining stationary, with legs crossed, and the hips a little above the knees (you could use a Buddhist *zafu* cushion for help with this posture).

With perseverance, you will find that your sense of time passing will completely change. 'Mountains know another time, another rhythm. To be seated like a mountain is to have eternity before you.'[66] It is the right attitude for anyone who wants to enter into meditation. It is learning 'how to be, simply to be, without aim or purpose'.[67]

---

[65] Leloup, *Being Still*, 3.
[66] Ibid.
[67] Ibid.

Meditating like a mountain will also modify the rhythm of thought: you will learn to see without judging, 'as though you were giving to all that grows on the mountain the right to exist.'[68]

2 TO MEDITATE LIKE A POPPY (*PHUSIS*)

'Meditation is first of all a posture', but meditation is also an orientation, and this is what the poppy can teache us: 'to turn towards the sun, to turn from the depths [of ourselves] towards the light', towards beauty [*to kalon*], 'to make of meditation the inspiration of all [our] strength and vigour.'[69]

You will also learn from the poppy that in order to maintain this position the flower has to have a straight stem, and so you will begin to straighten your spine.

The poppy is also fragile, and its blossom soon fades. So it is necessary not only to blossom, but also to wither. As the mountain gives us a sense of eternity, so the poppy gives us a sense of time. Thus

---

[68] Leloup, *Being Still*, 3.
[69] Leloup, *Being Still*, 4. As with 'meditating like a mountain', my accounts of 'meditating like a poppy' and 'meditation like an ocean' (below) draw directly on the poetically delightful phrasing of Leloup's exposition of the art of meditating.

you will learn to meditate without 'purpose or profit, but for the simple pleasure of being and of loving the light'.[70]

3 To Meditate Like an Ocean (*PSUCHÊ*)

Meditation is adopting a good posture and a proper frame of mind, but it is also learning to listen to your own breathing, and this is what the ocean teaches.

You will learn to harmonise your own breath with the great breathing of the waves. You inhale, you exhale ... then you are inhaled and you are exhaled. Let your own breath bear you up.

You may at first lose your everyday consciousness, or feel that you are floating. But soon your attention will no longer dwell within the rhythm of your breathing, and you will learn that to meditate is to simply breathe deeply, to just let be the breath's ebb and flow.

You will also realise that thoughts come and go, like foam washing around you. Listening to your breathing will enable you to become deeply aware of the impressions produced by the *hêgemonikon*.

---

[70] Leloup, *Being Still*, 5.

4 To Meditate Like a Sage (*nous*)

With the meditation of the Sage, you will enter into a new and higher awareness, the awareness of the *logos* which manifests itself in the 'intimate exchange of all things' but that 'cannot be grasped by all things'.[71]

Heraclitus deeply inspired the physics of the Stoics, and thus it is very important to understand the meaning of the word *logos* as he used it. Translators of the Gospels usually render *logos* as 'the word', but this translation does not help us much. Philosophers often use the term 'discourses'. This is not wrong, but this kind of linear comprehension of Heraclitus leaves us unsatisfied. How should we understand the *logos* in Greek? 'Logos', meaning 'word' or 'discourse', has its etymological root in the concept of *gathering*. *Legein* means first 'to gather' or 'to pick'. It was only with the development of classical Greek that *logos* came to mean 'to speak', or 'to say something'. But even around 270 BCE the poet Moschus of Syracuse was still writing *aglaien rhodou legein*, which translates as 'to pick the bloom of a rose'.

---

[71] Leloup, *Being Still*, 9.

Heraclitus invites us 'to pick the bloom'. The listening is also contemplation, which implies the absence of direction. An oriented listening, to the contrary, is a listening of the known, of the thought, of the mind, of memory, of habit. Other traditions use the term 'ego'.

Marcus Aurelius in his *Meditations* describes this exercise as follows:

> There are three things of which you are composed: body, breath, and mind. Of these, the first two are your own in so far it is your duty to take care of them; but only the third is your own in the full sense.
>
> So if you will put away from yourself—that is to say, from your mind—
>
> (1) all that others do or say
>
> (2) all that you yourself have done or said
>
> (3) all that troubles you with regard to the future
>
> (4) all that belonging to the body which envelops you and the breath conjoined with it [which] is attached to you independently of your will
>
> (5) all that the vortex whirling around outside you sweeps in its wake, so that the power of your mind
>
> —thus delivered from the bonds of fate, *may live a pure and unfettered life alone with itself, doing what is*

just, desiring what comes to pass, and saying what is true—

if I say, you will put away from your governing faculty—

(6) all that accretes to it from the affections of the body
(7) all that lies in the future or in time gone by

—and make yourself, in Empedocles' words, *'a well-rounded sphere rejoicing in the solitude around it'*, and strive to live only the life that is your own, that is to say, your present life, then you will be able to pass at least the time that is left to you until you die in calm and kindliness, and as one who is at peace with the guardian-spirit that dwells within him.[72]

Remaining in this state of listening, of openness, in every circumstance, is making yourself *'a well rounded sphere rejoicing in the solitude around it'*. Meditating is then worshiping the universe. Worshiping the universe is discovering that nothing belongs to us, but everything belongs to Nature, to the *logos*. This is abandoning our 'human, all too

---

[72] *Meditations*, 12.3. (trans. Hard, typographically modified).

human' self-centred point of view, what Christian orthodox tradition calls 'sacrifice', and what Buddhist philosophy calls 'detachment'.

That is the very living incorporation of the motto 'living according to nature' as Zeno stated, or 'living according to the experience of nature' as expressed by Chrysippus. Meditators all around the world do not search for extraordinary psychical states, they are simply listening to the *logos*, to what is.

IV Concluding thoughts

It is important to remember that in this short essay I have tried to give only an overview of Stoic meditative practices.

Some may criticise the extensive use I have made of Pierre Hadot's theories: I recently learnt that they are the subject of controversy, especially regarding his interpretation of the theory of knowledge and the treatment of impressions.

I nevertheless chose to rely on Hadot, because I felt when reading his work that there is some sort of spirituality which arises from it. Furthermore, in my view, his interpretation of 'impressions' can be easily incorporated in a comprehensive meditation system.

I myself experienced an appreciable inner growth on my way to understanding these practices, especially when I discovered the early traditions of the Desert Fathers. Indeed, early Christians drew deep inspiration from the ancient philosophers, including, most likely, Stoics and Platonists. We should be cognisant that Arrian's *Encheiridion*, for instance, has been used by Christians, after having been heavily modified for their daily practice, and was even used later to evangelise people in China.

I am aware that it would be possible to attempt a reconstruction of some core Stoic teachings using Cassian collations of the works of Jean-Yves Leloup,[73] especially bearing in mind that this method would have the advantage of relying upon what I believe to be the sole genuine authentic way of teaching the art of living well.

I should conclude that my Buddhist studies have been of great help, especially as far as the meditation techniques are concerned, and it is interesting to note that British psychologist and author David Fontana remarks that although meditation techniques developed in many different cultures (and not only in oriental ones), the techniques in themselves are similar everywhere. That is why early Christians also focused on breathing in order to develop attention.

I hope that you enjoyed this essay, and above all that it will be of practical help to you.

---

[73] That is, following the codification methods adopted by St John Cassian in his works the *Institutions* and the *Conferences*.

Spiritual Stoic Exercises
Elen Buzaré
Published by Lulu 2011
© 2011 Elen Buzaré
ISBN 978–1–4466–0811–1 (hardback)
ISBN 978–1–4466–0813–5 (paperback)

Typeset in Minion Pro by Keith Seddon using Microsoft Word 2007. Proofs checked and reviewed in Portable Document Format created using open source PDFCreator 1.2.0.

NOTE ON THE TYPEFACES

Main text is set in Minion Pro, designed by Robert Slimbach

Adobe informs us: 'Minion Pro is inspired by classical, old style typefaces of the late Renaissance, a period of elegant, beautiful, and highly readable type designs. Minion Pro combines the aesthetic and functional qualities that make text type highly readable with the versatility of OpenType digital technology, yielding unprecedented flexibility and typographic control, whether for lengthy text or display settings.'

(Abridged from
http://store1.adobe.com/type/browser/html/readmes/MinionProReadMe.html)

Display text is set in Fontin Sans, designed by Jos Buivenga of the exljbris Font Foundry

Fontin Sans is a classic sans serif typeface suitable for display and text, free for personal and commercial use, available from http://www.exljbris.com/fontinsans.html